Research & Resources
In Support of *This We Believe*

Association for Middle Level Education, formerly
National Middle School Association, Research Advisory Committee

Micki M. Caskey
P. Gayle Andrews
Penny A. Bishop
Robert M. Capraro
Mary Roe
Christopher Weiss

Association for Middle Level Education
Westerville, Ohio

Association for Middle Level Education
formerly National Middle School Association
4151 Executive Parkway, Suite 300, Westerville, Ohio 43081
tel: 800.528.6672   fax: 614.895.4750   www.amle.org

AMLE.

ISBN: 978-1-56090-234-8

Foreword

Unlike any time in recent history, middle level education is now widely recognized as critical for the learning, growth, and success of young adolescents. Educators, policymakers, business leaders, and parents reinforce the importance of ensuring that every 10- to 15-year-old receives a high-quality educational experience. While the characteristics of effective middle grades schools today reflect the philosophy and concepts identified for these schools years ago, it is through the work of researchers that we have opened more doors to student learning.

The Association for Middle Level Education, formerly National Middle School Association, is pleased to present this updated edition of *Research and Resources in Support of This We Believe*. This companion document to the fourth edition of *This We Believe: Keys to Educating Young Adolescents* reinforces earlier research and updates the findings on the 16 characteristics of effective middle grades schools. It not only underscores our beliefs but expands our understandings. It is an essential resource for every individual who works with and for young adolescents.

We wish to offer special thanks to the members of the association's Research Advisory Committee: Micki M. Caskey (chair), P. Gayle Andrews, Penny A. Bishop, Robert M. Capraro, Mary Roe, and Christopher Weiss. These individuals have devoted countless hours to the identification and summarization of the research studies and resources found in this document. Micki Caskey deserves special recognition for her leadership in bringing this document to completion.

The AMLE Board of Trustees

Contents

Contents continued

Preface

The second edition of *Research and Resources in Support of This We Believe* serves as a complement and companion to *This We Believe: Keys to Educating Young Adolescents* (National Middle School Association, 2010). Not only does this edition build on the research base summarized in the original *Research and Resources in Support of This We Believe* (Anfara et al., 2003), but it also updates the research on the 16 characteristics advanced in *This We Believe*. We developed the book as a tool for middle level administrators, teachers, policy makers, and other interested stakeholders—those who intend to create and sustain effective schools for young adolescents. It is our sincere hope that educators will use the research summaries and recommended resources included in this book to inform their decisions related to policies, programs, and practices for educating young adolescents.

This edition of *Research and Resources* includes four major parts. Part One, Introduction, offers a rationale for the book, a definition of research, and an overview of recent middle grades research. Part Two, Middle Grades Research: Past and Present, presents key research that addressed the tenets outlined in *This We Believe: Developmentally Responsive Middle Schools* (National Middle School Association, 1995) and *Turning Points: Preparing American Youth for the 21st Century* (Carnegie Council on Adolescent Development, 1989). We selected for inclusion those studies that link the middle school concept to improved student performance. Part Three, Research and Resources on *This We Believe* Characteristics, provides research summaries for (a) curriculum, instruction, and assessment; (b) leadership and organization; and (c) culture and community. This part also includes annotated references of important research studies for each of the 16 characteristics that warrant attention as well as a set of recommended resources. Both are excellent starting points for those who wish to deepen their understanding of middle grades research and practice. The book concludes with Part Four, Middle Grades Research: Future Directions, which suggests the next steps to expand and enhance the research base in middle level education.

References

Anfara, V. A., Jr., Andrews, P. G., Hough, D. L., Mertens, S. B., Mizelle, N. B., & White, G. P. (2003). *Research and resources in support of This We Believe.* Westerville, OH: National Middle School Association.

Carnegie Council on Adolescent Development. (1989). *Turning points: Preparing American youth for the 21ˢᵗ century.* New York: Carnegie Corporation.

National Middle School Association. (1995). *This we believe: Developmentally responsive middle schools.* Columbus, OH: Author.

National Middle School Association. (2010). *This we believe: Keys to educating young adolescents.* Westerville, OH: Author.

Part I
Introduction

The Association for Middle level Education, formerly National Middle School Association, (2010) presents a clear vision and conceptual framework to advance the development of effective school programs and educational practices for young adolescents in *This We Believe: Keys to Educating Young Adolescents*. This position paper is an invaluable, multifaceted resource that serves well as a professional guidebook, evaluative tool, and reference point for future research endeavors.

Today more than ever, educators, policymakers, parents, community members, and other stakeholders look for evidence as a basis for making educational decisions. They rightfully want to know "What works?" and look to research for answers to this central question. This growing interest in and need for research evidence is significant and timely, especially when considering what is most effective for educating young adolescents.

Research and Resources in Support of This We Believe (2nd ed.) responds to the central question, "What works?" as well as other questions that are relevant to the education of young adolescents. Following a brief overview of research, this volume provides succinct research summaries on the key characteristics outlined in *This We Believe: Keys to Educating Young Adolescents* (NMSA/AMLE, 2010). These summaries communicate what research says about middle grades education. Accompanying the research summaries are annotated references and recommended resources intended for educators and policymakers' use when considering policies and making decisions for schools and school districts. In short, the purpose of this book is to share summaries of research and relevant resources that researchers and practitioners alike can use.

The research base that supports the middle school concept and middle grades education has continued to grow. For example, the NMSA Research Advisory Committee summarized important middle grades research in *Research and Resources in Support of This We Believe* (Anfara et al., 2003) to accompany *This We Believe: Successful Schools for Young Adolescents* (NMSA, 2003). In addition to this noteworthy and useful contribution to middle grades education, numerous research articles have appeared in *Research in Middle Level Education Online, Middle Grades Research Journal, The Journal of Early Adolescence,* and other peer-reviewed journals. Similarly, research studies have filled *The Handbook of Research in Middle Level Education* series and the *Middle Level Education Research Annuals.* For example, *An International Look at Educating Young Adolescents* (Mertens, Anfara, & Roney, 2009) presented comparative research from 14 countries, while *Connecting with Parents and Families* (Caskey, 2009) shared a collection of up-to-date topical research. Most recently, reports have documented the significance of the middle grades for keeping students on track for high school graduation (Balfanz, Herzog, & Mac Iver, 2007) and beyond (ACT, 2008). Certainly, the expanding research base has contributed significantly to what we know about middle grades education.

> The expanding research base has contributed significantly to what we know about middle grades education.

What is Research?

Anfara and colleagues (2003) offered the following operational definition of research: "Research is an original work that reports the methods and findings from the systematic collection and analysis of empirical data" (p. 2). We adopted this definition to guide the selection of research articles, reviews of research, and research summaries for inclusion in the second edition of *Research and Resources in Support of This We Believe.* Using this definition as a lens allowed us to contribute to the knowledge base with the same level of integrity.

Documenting the Research

In *R³ = Research, Rhetoric, and Reality: A Study of Studies,* Hough (2003) identified, analyzed, and categorized the middle grades research studies conducted from 1991–2002 that addressed the research needs advanced in *A 21ˢᵗ Century Research Agenda: Issues, Topics, & Questions Guiding Inquiry into Middle Level Theory and Practice* (NMSA, 1997) and *This We Believe: Developmentally Responsive Middle Schools* (NMSA, 1995). Across this 12-year period, researchers published 3,717 studies on an array of topics in the field of middle grades education. The research studies were disseminated in a variety of formats including dissertations, ERIC journal articles and documents, and conference presentations at the annual meetings of the American Educational Research Association and National Middle School Association. Research methodologies used also varied with approximately 65% qualitative, 15% quantitative, and 20% action research methodologies. Hough reported few meta-analyses and experimental designs.

Anfara and colleagues (2003) noted, "Virtually no middle level education studies were replications of prior effects" (p. 3). In other words, middle grades researchers have not used the same research design, data collection methods, and analyses to examine an issue or topic. This is an important issue in middle grades education research because replication is necessary to validate prior research findings and strengthen the knowledge base.

Calling for Additional Middle Grades Education Research

Though the middle grades research base has continued to grow, additional research and specific types of research need to be conducted. Anfara and colleagues (2003) suggested, "There is an urgency regarding research in this area" (p. 4). Similarly, Mertens (2006) asserted, "The most critical issue facing middle level education today is the paucity of good, reliable research studies that have been able to demonstrate, quantitatively or qualitatively, the link between the components of the middle school philosophy and any type of teaching or learning outcome" (p. 2). In sum, the field of middle grades education needs more research including the replication of previously conducted studies and the development of original, well-designed research studies.

References

ACT. (2008). *The forgotten middle: Ensuring that all students are on target for college and career readiness before high school.* Iowa City, IA: Author.

Anfara, V. A., Jr., Andrews, P. G., Hough, D. L., Mertens, S. B., Mizelle, N. B., & White, G. P. (2003). *Research and resources in support of This We Believe.* Westerville, OH: National Middle School Association.

Balfanz, R., Herzog, L., & Mac Iver, D. (2007). Preventing student disengagement and keeping students on the graduation path in urban middle grade schools: Early identification and effective interventions. *Educational Psychologist, 42*(4), 223–235.

Caskey, M. M. (Ed.). (2009). *Middle level education research annual: Connecting with parents and families.* Westerville, OH: National Middle School Association.

Hough, D. L. (2003). *R3 = Research, rhetoric, and reality: A study of studies addressing NMSA's 21st Century Research Agenda and This We Believe.* Westerville, OH: National Middle School Association.

Mertens, S. B. (2006). *A proposal for establishing a national middle level research project.* A research white paper. Retrieved July 27, 2009, from http://www.rmle.pdx.edu/docs/MLERNationalMLProjectWhitePaper.pdf

Mertens, S. B., Anfara, V A., Jr., & Roney, K. (Eds.). (2009.) *An international look at educating young adolescents.* Charlotte, NC: Information Age Publishing.

National Middle School Association. (1995). *This we believe: Developmentally responsive middle schools.* Columbus, OH: Author.

National Middle School Association. (1997). *A 21st century research agenda: Issues, topics, & questions guiding inquiry into middle level theory & practice.* Columbus, OH: Author.

National Middle School Association. (2003). *This we believe: Successful schools for young adolescents.* Westerville, OH: Author.

National Middle School Association. (2010). *This we believe: Keys to educating young adolescents.* Westerville, OH: Author.

Part II

Middle Level Research: Past and Present

The research base that supports middle grades education and the middle school concept is vitally important. Not only do research findings influence perceptions of current middle grades programs and practices, but they also provide concrete evidence of effectiveness. Leaders in middle grades education can draw on a solid research foundation—decades of disciplined inquiry—to build effective middle grades schools. Certainly research confirms that middle grades education is a significant and distinct level of schooling with its own tenets and characteristics.

High-quality research that examined the impact of the middle school concept on student achievement and socio-emotional development are worthy of review for a number of reasons. First, this research documents an explicit link between the middle school concept and improved student outcomes. Second, these studies consider multiple programmatic components of the middle school concept and reform efforts, rather than a single dimension. Third, they report generalizable findings and serve as models of replicable research designs. Specific studies for consideration in this section include those conducted by Lee and Smith (1993); Felner and associates (1997); Mertens, Flowers, and Mulhall (1998); Backes, Ralston, and Ingwalson (1999); and Mertens and Flowers (2006).

Lee and Smith (1993) investigated the effect of restructured middle schools' attendance on the achievement, engagement, and social stratification of students. They drew a subsample of 8,845 eighth graders in 377 public, Catholic, and independent middle grades schools from the *National Educational Longitudinal Study of 1988* (NELS:88). The researchers examined the impact of middle school restructuring (i.e., reduced departmentalization,

> Students who attended schools with fewer eighth grade peers showed greater levels of academic engagement

more heterogeneous grouping, more team teaching, and a composite restructuring measure) on eighth grade students' achievement, engagement with academic work, and at-risk behaviors. Results of their investigation demonstrated positive effects of restructuring for both student achievement and engagement. Findings revealed that reduced departmentalization and heterogeneous grouping of students was associated with social equity in achievement among students. Moreover, students who attended schools with fewer eighth grade peers showed greater levels of academic engagement and more equitably distributed achievement outcomes. Lee and Smith summarized, "Our results lend empirical support to the movement to restructure schools attended by early adolescents" (p. 182).

Felner and associates (1997) evaluated the impact of implementing the recommendations set forth in *Turning Points* (Carnegie Council on Adolescent Development, 1989)—a comprehensive middle school reform initiative—on student academic achievement, socio-emotional development, and behavioral adjustment. During the 1990–1992 school years, Felner's research team collected data from 31 Illinois middle schools representing a range of demographic characteristics including urban, suburban, and rural settings. Their study focused on four structural changes in middle schools: (1) teaming with common planning time, (2) small number of students per team, (3) frequent advisory periods, and (4) appropriate educational practices for young adolescents. They developed a definition of implementation that specified high, partial, and low levels of implementation of these structural changes. The principal data source was a set of annual surveys (i.e., High Performance Learning Communities Assessments) administered to teachers, school staff, students, administrators, and parents. Secondary data sources included achievement test scores (reading, language arts, and mathematics) and student records.

The results indicated that students in highly implemented schools had higher achievement scores than students in partial or low-implemented schools. Results also showed students in highly implemented schools experienced fewer behavioral problems (e.g., aggression) and reported higher levels of self-esteem as well as less fear and worry. These findings led Felner and colleagues (1997) to conclude that the aforementioned positive outcomes "are not obtained until implementation is quite mature, comprehensive, and conducted with a high degree of fidelity" (p. 67).

Mertens, Flowers, and Mulhall (1998), researchers from the Center for Prevention Research and Development (CPRD) at the University of Illinois, studied comprehensive middle school reform in Michigan. Using the School Improvement Self-Study, baseline and longitudinal data was collected from 155 middle grades schools participating in the reform initiative (i.e., Michigan Middle Start Initiative) funded by the W. K. Kellogg Foundation. Administrators, teachers, and students completed the self-study surveys— based on recommendations of *Turning Points* (Carnegie Council on Adolescent Development, 1989)—in 1994–95 and 1996–97. The research team developed 24 scales to measure components of reform including curriculum, instruction, school climate, school organization, professional development, and parent involvement.

Importantly, Mertens and colleagues (1998) linked data from the self-study surveys with student achievement data, which allowed them to measure the impact of middle school reform on student performance. They designed the study to compare 21 Middle Start "grant" schools with the 134 "non-grant" schools. While both groups of schools engaged in self-study, only the grant schools received funding, professional development, on-site support, and networking opportunities to support the reform initiative. Results indicated that students in the grant schools significantly outperformed those in the non-grant schools on both reading and mathematics achievement tests (i.e., Michigan Education Assessment Program).

Results revealed other outcomes for students and teachers in the Middle Start grant schools. Students reported higher levels of stress to succeed academically but also reported more positive self-esteem and academic efficacy as well as feeling safer at their schools. Teachers reported using more effective middle school practices, working more successfully with young adolescents, and connecting more with parents. Mertens and colleagues (1998) called upon schools to use their Self-Study data to (a) engage in ongoing conversations about school improvement, (b) set school improvement goals, and (c) monitor progress toward those goals.

In another study, Backes, Ralston, and Ingwalson (1999) examined the effect of middle school practices on student achievement in North Dakota schools participating in the Middle Grades School State Policy Initiative— known as BRIDGES schools. The researchers designed the study to compare the impact of implementing middle school practices (i.e., *Turning Points* recommendations) on BRIDGES schools and non-BRIDGES schools. Results indicated that student achievement (as measured by composite grade equivalent scores from grades six to eight) was higher in BRIDGES schools than non-BRIDGES schools in the areas of reading vocabulary, language mechanics, study skills, science, and social studies. While Non-BRIDGES schools had higher student achievement in language expression and math computations, concepts, and applications, there was no difference in reading comprehension and spelling. In sum, schools implementing *Turning Points* recommendations offered some promising results with regard to student achievement.

In a more recent research study, Mertens and Flowers (2006), CPRD researchers, examined the effectiveness of Middle Start—a regional comprehensive school reform initiative (see Mertens et al., 1998)—that focused on implementation of middle school practices. The researchers employed a quasi-experimental design with a sample of three groups of schools (i.e., Comprehensive School Improvement schools, Comprehensive School Reform Demonstration schools, and control group schools). They collected data from each school group using the School Improvement Self-Study—a set of teacher, student, administrator, and parent surveys.

> The schools engaged in teaming with high common planning time had the greatest achievement gains over time.

Results indicated that schools with high levels of middle school practices (e.g., interdisciplinary teaming) demonstrate greater student achievement outcomes than schools with lower levels of middle school practices. In addition, poverty schools participating in the Middle Start comprehensive school reform initiative showed greater achievement gains over time when compared to more affluent schools that participated in the reform initiative. Further, after the initiative's grant funding ended, Middle Start schools continued to exhibit gains in student achievement, though gains in team and classroom practices were minimal. Mertens and Flowers concluded, "Overall, the schools engaged in teaming wi th high common planning time had the greatest achievement gains over time" (p. 22).

Results of these five major research studies provide middle level educators, policymakers, and others with solid evidence regarding the effectiveness of the middle school concept. Certainly, these studies are significant and worthy of more attention. Not only do they document significant findings about middle grades practices, but they also serve as models for middle grades researchers.

References

Anfara, V. A., Jr., Andrews, P. G., Hough, D. L., Mertens, S. B., Mizelle, N. B., & White, G. P. (2003). *Research and resources in support of This We Believe.* Westerville, OH: National Middle School Association.

Backes, J., Ralston, A., & Ingwalson, G. (1999). Middle level reform: The impact on student achievement. *Research in Middle Level Education Quarterly, 22*(3), 43–57.

Carnegie Council on Adolescent Development. (1989). *Turning points: Preparing American youth for the 21ˢᵗ century.* New York: Carnegie Corporation.

Felner, R. D., Jackson, A. W., Kasak, D., Mulhall, P., Brand, S., & Flowers, N. (1997). The impact of school reform for the middle years: Longitudinal study of a network engaged in Turning Points-based comprehensive school transformation. *Phi Delta Kappan, 78*(7), 528–532, 541–550.

Lee, V. E., & Smith, J. B. (1993). Effects of school restructuring on achievement and engagement of middle-grade students. *Sociology of Education, 66*(3), 164–187.

Mertens, S. B., & Flowers, N. (2006). Middle Start's impact on comprehensive middle school reform. *Middle Grades Research Journal, 1*(1), 1–26.

Mertens, S. B., Flowers, N., & Mulhall, P. (1998). *The Middle Start initiative, phase I: A longitudinal analysis of Michigan middle-level schools.* Center for Prevention Research and Development, University of Illinois.

Part III

Research & Resources on *This We Believe* Characteristics

Curriculum, Instruction, & Assessment

Research Summary

Compelling evidence for effective curriculum, instruction, and assessment for young adolescents reveals that teaching and learning strategies employed in middle grades classrooms should be as diverse, varied, and lively as the students themselves.

Purposeful learning is a key to engaging middle schoolers. Rogers and Freiberg (1994) described learning as a continuum, with the learning of isolated facts at one end and "significant, meaningful, experiential learning" at the other (p. 36). Students are most interested and engaged when they experience hands-on activities in authentic contexts (Needels & Knapp, 1994; Randler & Hulde, 2007). Service-learning "connects schools and communities in a deliberate effort to construct learning opportunities for youth" (Honig, Kahne, & McLaughlin, 2001, p. 1011), providing benefits for student achievement (e.g., Melchior, 1997); fostering global pro-environmental attitudes and behaviors (Schneller, 2008); and diminishing rates of school suspension, school dropout, and school failure (e.g., Allen, Philliber, Herrling, & Kuperminc, 1997).

To arrive at a relevant and active curriculum, students and teachers hold joint responsibility for their interactions and learning (Nesin, 2005). Integrative curriculum design promises much for middle grades teachers who wish to develop classroom curriculum that will encourage young adolescents to engage actively in their learning (Andrews, 2008; Dowden, 2007) (cf. Beane, 1993, 1997, 2005). Developing curriculum around events and issues requires a unique curricular process that allows teachers to plan in real time as events unfold and issues become salient. As a result, teachers need to adopt a generative approach to curriculum planning that involves responsive and reflective practices (Virtue, 2007).

The varied learning and teaching approaches in effective middle grades classrooms are often characterized by an inquiry-oriented, problem-based framework—one that calls for long-term, interdisciplinary, student-centered lessons grounded in real-world issues (Krajcik & Czerniak, 2007). Each young adolescent is unique, with a particular cultural, experiential, and personal background and a distinctive array of learning styles, interests, talents, and skills (e.g., Brighton, 2007; Delpit, 1995; Dunn, 1996; Lasley & Matczynski, 1997). No single teaching method will work for every student; in fact, no single method will work for any one student every day. Instead, research points to the positive impact on student achievement of using varied, appropriate, and differentiated strategies for learning and teaching (Beecher & Sweeny, 2008; Brighton, Hertberg, Moon, Tomlinson, & Callahan, 2005; Brimijoin, 2001; Tieso, 2002; Tomlinson, Brimijoin, & Narvaez, 2008; Tomlinson & McTighe, 2006). Diverse instructional strategies can lead to more independent and aware students (Gutstein, 2003), especially when skillful teachers differentiate for students' capacities and interests (Tomlinson & McTighe).

Assessment of such complex learning requires a balance of formative and summative strategies to inform instruction, advance learning, and provide evaluative data (Chappuis & Stiggins, 2008; Heritage, 2007). Considering assessment and evaluation in schools over the last 40 years, each generation has brought new calls for accountability and added layers of testing for students so that schools now have district-wide, state-wide, national, and international assessment programs, all operating simultaneously (Stiggins, 2002). Although these forms of summative assessment can be useful, formative assessment plays a critical role in both teaching and learning. For formative assessment to function effectively in a middle grades classroom, it is important that (a) students be actively engaged in learning; (b) teachers systematically use the results of the formative assessment to make adjustments in their teaching; (c) students learn to self-assess so that they will understand the main purpose of their learning; and (d) teachers give feedback that tells students how they can improve and does not make comparisons among students.

Engaging students in meaningful learning experiences requires educators who understand the nature of young adolescents and who have been specifically prepared to teach in the middle grades. Research supports that fully prepared middle grades teachers are critical to the academic success of their students. In general, this proposition is supported through the work of Darling-Hammond (e.g., 2000, 2006, 2008) and Darling-Hammond, Chung, and Frelow (2002). More specifically, for middle grades educators, researchers at the Center for Prevention Research and Development (CPRD) provide evidence about the critical connection between appropriate teacher preparation programs and student achievement. Flowers, Mertens, and Mulhall (1999) and Mertens, Flowers, and Mulhall (2002) indicated that teachers who participate in specialized middle grades teacher education programs are more likely to be involved in effective team and classroom practices. Therefore, those teachers have the potential to effect greater gains in student learning, as defined by student achievement scores (Mertens et al.).

> To arrive at a relevant and active curriculum, students and teachers hold joint responsibility for their interactions and learning.

A review of the status of middle grades licensure and certification reveals that 46 states plus the District of Columbia offer some form of middle grades licensure, but confirms that fewer than 50% of the states require specific licensure to teach in the middle grades and certification areas overlap significantly within states (Gaskill, 2007; McEwin, 2007). These circumstances undermine the development of quality middle grades teacher education programs within individual states and across the nation and, ultimately, limit the number of fully prepared middle grades teachers (McEwin, Smith, & Dickinson, 2003). Such specialization is important given, that teacher quality is more related to increases in student achievement, particularly in reading and mathematics, than teachers' education levels (Anfara et al., 2003; Darling-Hammond, 2000).

References

Allen, J. P., Philliber, S., Herrling, S., & Kuperminc, G. P. (1997). Preventing teen pregnancy and academic failure: Experimental evaluation of a developmentally based approach. *Child Development, 64,* 729–742.

Andrews, P. G. (2008). Centering on students in the middle grades curriculum. *Middle School Journal, 40*(2), 44–51.

Anfara, V. A., Jr., Andrews, P. G., Hough, D. L., Mertens, S. B., Mizelle, N. B., & White, G. P. (2003). *Research and resources in support of This We Believe.* Westerville, OH: National Middle School Association.

Beane, J. A. (1993). *A middle school curriculum: From rhetoric to reality* (2nd ed.). Columbus, OH: National Middle School Association.

Beane, J. A. (1997). *Curriculum integration: Designing the core of democratic education.* New York: Teachers College Press.

Beane, J. A. (2005). *A reason to teach: Creating classrooms of dignity and hope.* Portsmouth, NH: Heinemann.

Beecher, M., & Sweeny, S. (2008). Closing the achievement gap with curriculum enrichment and differentiation: One school's story. *Journal of Advanced Academics, 19,* 502–530.

Brighton, C., Hertberg, H., Moon, T., Tomlinson, C., & Callahan, C. (2005). *The feasibility of high-end learning in a diverse middle school. Research Monograph RM05210.* Charlottesville, VA: National Research Center on the Gifted and Talented.

Brighton, K. (2007). *Coming of age: The education and development of young adolescents.* Westerville, OH: National Middle School Association.

Brimijoin, K. (2001). *Expertise in differentiation: A pre-service and in-service teacher make their way.* A dissertation presented to the Curry School of Education, University of Virginia. Charlottesville, VA: University of Virginia.

Chappuis, S., & Stiggins, R. (2008). Finding balance: Assessment in the middle school classroom. *Middle Ground, 12*(2), 12–15.

Darling-Hammond, L. (2000). Teacher quality and student achievement: A review of state policy evidence. *Education Policy Analysis Archives, 8*(1). Retrieved August 12, 2009, from http://epaa.asu/edu/epaa/v8n1/

Darling-Hammond, L. (2006). *Powerful teacher education: Lessons from exemplary programs.* San Francisco: Jossey-Bass.

Darling-Hammond, L. (2008). The case for university-based teacher education. In M. Cochran-Smith, S. Fieman-Nemser, & D. J. McIntyre (Eds.), *Handbook of research on teacher education: Enduring questions in changing contexts* (pp. 249–257). New York: Routledge.

Darling-Hammond, L., Chung, R., & Frelow, F. (2002). Variation in teacher preparation: How well do different pathways prepare teachers to teach? *Journal of Teacher Education,53,* 286–302.

Delpit, L. (1995). *Other people's children: Cultural conflict in the classroom.* New York: The New Press.

Dowden, T. (2007). Relevant, challenging, integrative, and exploratory curriculum design: Perspectives from theory and practice for middle level schooling in Australia. *The Australian Educational Researcher, 34*(2), 51–72.

Dunn, R. (1996). *How to implement and supervise a learning styles program.* Alexandria, VA: Association for Supervision and Curriculum Development.

Flowers, N., Mertens, S., & Mulhall, P. (1999). The impact of teaming: Five research-based outcomes of teaming. *Middle School Journal, 31*(2), 57–60.

Gaskill, P. E. (2007). *The current status of middle grades teaching credentials: Executive summary.* Retrieved August 15, 2009, from http://www. peggygaskill.com/images/Executive%20Summary-March%202007.pdf

Gutstein, E. (2003). Teaching and learning mathematics for social justice in an urban, Latino school. *Journal for Research in Mathematics Education, 34*(1), 37–73.

Heritage, M. (2007). Formative assessment: What do teachers need to know and do? *Phi Delta Kappan, 89,* 140–145.

Honig, M. I., Kahne, J., & McLaughlin, M. W. (2001). School-community connections: Strengthening opportunity to learn and opportunity to teach. In V. Richardson (Ed.), *Handbook of research on teaching* (4th ed.) (pp. 998–1028). Washington, DC: American Educational Research Association.

Krajcik, J., & Czerniak C. (2007). *Teaching science in elementary and middle school: A project-based approach.* New York: Routledge.

Lasley, T., & Matczynski, T. (1997). *Strategies for teaching in a diverse society: Instructional models.* Belmont, CA: Wadsworth.

McEwin, C. K. (2007). *Middle level teacher certification/licensure patterns by state.* Retrieved August 14, 2009, from http://www.nmsa.org/ProfessionalPreparation/CertificationLicensurebyState/tabid/1235/Default.aspx

McEwin, C. K., Smith, T. W., & Dickinson, T. S. (2003). In P. G. Andrews & V. A. Anfara, Jr., (Eds.), *Leaders for a movement: Professional preparation and development of middle level teachers and administrators* (pp. 2–26). Greenwich, CT: Information Age.

Melchior, A. (1997). *National evaluation of Learn and Serve America school and community-based programs.* Waltham, MA: Center for Human Resources, Brandeis University.

Mertens, S. B., Flowers, N., & Mulhall, P. (2002). The relationship between middle-grades teacher certification and teaching practices. In V. A. Anfara, Jr., & S. L. Stacki (Eds.), *Middle school curriculum, instruction, and assessment* (pp. 119–138). Greenwich, CT: Information Age.

Needels, M., & Knapp, M. (1994). Teaching writing to children who are underserved. *Journal of Educational Psychology, 86,* 339–349.

Nesin, G. (2005). Students and teachers engaged in active learning. In T. O. Erb (Ed.), *This we believe in action: Implementing successful middle level schools* (pp. 53–62).Westerville, OH: National Middle School Association.

Randler, C., & Hulde, M. (2007). Hands-on versus teacher-centered experiments in soil ecology. *Research in Science & Technological Education, 25,* 329–338.

Rogers, C., & Freiberg, H. J. (1994). *Freedom to learn.* New York: Macmillan.

Schneller, A. J. (2008). Environmental service learning: Outcomes of innovative pedagogy in Baja California Sur, Mexico. *Environmental Education Research, 14,* 291–307.

Stiggins, R. J. (2002). Assessment crisis: The absence of assessment FOR learning. *Phi Delta Kappan, 83,* 758–765.

Tieso, C. (2002). *The effects of grouping and curricular practices on intermediate students' math achievement.* Research Monograph 02154. Storrs, CT: University of Connecticut, National Research Center on the Gifted and Talented.

Tomlinson, C., Brimijoin, K., & Narvaez, L. (2008). *The differentiated school: Making revolutionary changes in teaching and learning.* Alexandria, VA: Association for Supervision and Curriculum Development.

Tomlinson, C. A., & McTighe, J. (2006). *Integrating differentiated instruction and understanding by design: Connecting content and kids.* Alexandria, VA: Association for Supervision and Curriculum Development.

Virtue, D. C. (2007). Seizing teachable moments to develop integrative middle level curriculum. *Middle School Journal, 38*(4), 14–20.

Curriculum, Instruction, & Assessment Characteristics

Educators value young adolescents and are prepared to teach them. (Value Young Adolescents)

Annotated References

Anfara, V. A., Jr., & Beaumont-Schmidt, J. (2007). Defining the effectiveness of middle grades teachers. *Middle School Journal, 38*(5), 54–62.

In this research overview, Anfara and Beaumont-Schmidt examined what it means to be an effective middle grades teacher. The authors described the research on effective teaching characteristics, dividing them into content knowledge, pedagogical skills, classroom management, and student–teacher relationships. They compared this more general research with that specific to middle grades teaching and concluded that very little difference exists between researchers' definitions of effective teaching and effective middle grades teaching. The authors recommended that the field: (a) expand the definition of "highly qualified teachers;" (b) examine the impact of middle grades licensure; (c) apply a more multifaceted perspective to educational policy development; (d) consider the characteristics of effective teachers when hiring and providing professional development; and (e) encourage teachers to self-evaluate against the identified skills and attributes of effective teachers.

Mertens, S. B., Flowers, N., & Mulhall, P. (2002). The relationship between middle-grades teacher certification and teaching practices. In V. A. Anfara, Jr. & S. L. Stacki (Eds.), *Middle school curriculum, instruction, and assessment* (pp. 119–138). Greenwich, CT: Information Age.

Through a quantitative (descriptive and inferential) analysis of self-report survey data from 2001 teachers in 134 schools engaged in the Michigan Middle Start initiative, Mertens, Flowers, and Mulhall concluded that middle grades- and elementary-certified teachers were more likely to engage in classroom practices that are effective in teaching young adolescents than teachers without these certification levels. They found that settings where teaming and high levels of common planning time were present for all, teachers, regardless of certification, reported higher levels of effective team and classroom practices. Furthermore, schools where teaming and high levels of common planning time were the norm, the middle grades certified faculty reported the highest levels of effective team and classroom practices.

Van Zandt Allen, L., Ruebel, K. K., Greene, M. W., McDaniel, J. E., & Spencer, V. (2009). Putting *This We Believe* into action in performance-based teacher education. *Middle School Journal, 40*(3), 38–46.

In this article, Van Zandt Allen, Ruebel, Greene, McDaniel, and Spencer, tackled the question of effective middle grades teacher preparation through the lens of program accreditation. They summarized the review process as well as the corresponding NCATE/NMSA program standards and provided two examples of teacher candidate assessments that align with each standard. Additionally, the authors discussed typical challenges associated with the accreditation process, equipping teacher educators with a clear systems perspective of preparing teachers for the middle grades.

Students and teachers are engaged in active, purposeful learning. (Active Learning)

Annotated References

Bransford, J. D., Brown, A. L., & Cocking, R. R. (Eds.). (2003). *How people learn: Brain, mind, experience, and school: Expanded edition.* Washington, DC: National Academy Press.

The National Research Council's Committee on Developments in the Science of Learning reviewed developments in the science of learning from multiple fields of study including cognitive psychology, neuroscience, human development, social psychology, education, and anthropology. The Committee's report, *How People Learn: Brain, Mind, Experience, and School:*

Expanded Edition built on earlier editions and provided succinct overviews of each study's research methodology. *How People Learn* synthesized key research findings from hundreds of research studies within a framework focused on learners and learning and teachers and teaching. In addition to centering on research on human learning, the authors considered the implications of such research for instructional learning environments and explored the possibility for such research to help all individuals reach their fullest potential.

Nesin, G. (2005). Students and teachers engaged in active learning. In T. O. Erb (Ed.), *This we believe in action: Implementing successful middle level schools* (pp. 53–62).Westerville, OH: National Middle School Association.

In this chapter, Nesin noted that to foster active learning a safe and supportive classroom community must be in place. Citing reports from the National Research Council and other researchers, she indicated that students and teachers hold joint responsibility for their interactions and learning. The chapter addressed cognitive learning (including information about intelligence, building advanced concepts, transfer of learning, and metacognition) as well as social, moral and physical learning. Nesin also provided a set of implications for practice and examples that contrast passive and active learning.

Curriculum is challenging, exploratory, integrative, and relevant. (Challenging Curriculum)

Annotated References

Dowden, T. (2007). Relevant, challenging, integrative and exploratory curriculum design: Perspectives from theory and practice for middle level schooling in Australia. *The Australian Educational Researcher, 34*(2), 51–72.

Integrative curriculum design promises much for middle grades teachers who wish to develop classroom curriculum that will encourage young adolescents to engage actively in their learning (cf. Beane, 1993, 1997). Dowden examined the theory of the integrative and the multidisciplinary models of curriculum integration with respect to middle grades curriculum reform in Australian schools. The author traced a century of development of curriculum integration in the USA: from Dewey's Laboratory School a century ago to contemporary middle schooling.

Virtue, D. C. (2007). Seizing teachable moments to develop integrative middle level curriculum. *Middle School Journal, 38*(4), 14–20.

In this article, Virtue explicated the importance of curriculum that is relevant, challenging, integrative, and exploratory. He noted, however, that developing curriculum around events and issues such as these requires a unique curricular process that allows teachers to plan in real time as events unfold and issues become salient. He specified that teachers need to adopt a generative approach to curriculum planning that involves responsive and reflective practices.

Educators use multiple learning and teaching approaches. (Multiple Learning Approaches)

Annotated References

Krajcik, J., & Czerniak C. (2007). *Teaching science in elementary and middle school: A project-based approach.* New York: Routledge.

The need for a scientifically literate population who can apply scientific ideas to solve real-world problems in the 21st century has never been greater. Yet a growing disconnect exists between this need and the educational capacity to prepare them for solving problems. Krajcik and Czerniak organized their volume around the guiding principles of problem-based learning: long-term, interdisciplinary, student-centered lessons that are relevant to real-world issues and activities. They described how this research-based teaching approach engages all young learners—regardless of culture, race, or gender—in exploring important and meaningful questions through a process of investigation and collaboration. The authors detailed a dynamic process in which students ask questions, make predictions, design investigations, collect and analyze data, make products, and share ideas. Krajcik and Czerniak also presented a discussion of teaching with technology including the use of wireless handhelds, cameras, cell phones, wikis, and iPods. Additionally, they developed an accompanying website with strategies to support students in problem solving, planning, and carrying out investigations.

Gutstein, E. (2003). Teaching and learning mathematics for social justice in urban, Latino school. *Journal for Research in Mathematics Education, 34,* 37–73.

Gutstein, a middle grades teacher who implemented a National Council of Teachers of Mathematics standards-based curriculum, discussed the role of teaching and learning mathematics in an urban, Latino classroom. He explained how his students "read the world" by means of mathematics and at the same time developed mathematical power. In the article, Gutstein described a series of real-world projects that changed students' attitudes toward mathematics as the issues of culture, justice, social equity, and diversity emerged. Through these diverse strategies, students became increasingly independent and aware.

Varied and ongoing assessments advance learning as well as measure it. (Varied Assessments)

Annotated References

Chappuis, S., & Stiggins, R. (2008). Finding balance: Assessment in the middle school classroom. *Middle Ground, 12*(2), 12–15.

Chappuis and Stiggins highlighted that summative and formative assessments are viewed as a balanced classroom assessment system where neither of the two components is overused or underused. After defining summative and formative assessment, they asserted that these assessments work together to generate combined effects that are greater than the sum of the individual parts. In this article, Chappuis and Stiggins described the five indicators of sound classroom assessment practice: (1) Why access? (2) Access what? (3) Access how? (4) Communicate how? and (5) Involve students how? The authors included an audit checklist for teachers to measure their balance of classroom assessments. They also provided a useful set of resources.

Heritage, M. (2007). Formative assessment: What do teachers need to know and do? *Phi Delta Kappan, 89,* 140–145.

Heritage described the use of formative assessment as a means to enlighten teaching and learning in schools and discussed the accountability environment which focuses on summative assessment. She explored formative assessment as a means to inform effective instruction by providing information on student needs and progress. She explained several formative assessment strategies including on-the-fly assessment, planned-for interaction, and curriculum-embedded assessment. Heritage also detailed the four core elements of formative assessment: identifying the gap, feedback, student involvement, and learning progressions. Finally, she considered critical components of teacher knowledge and the skills teachers needed to implement formative assessment.

Recommended Resources

Anfara, V. A., Jr., Andrews, P. G., & Mertens, S. B. (Eds.). (2005). *The encyclopedia of middle grades education.* Greenwich, CT: Information Age.

Anfara, V. A., Jr., & Stacki, S. L. (2002). *Middle school curriculum, instruction, and assessment.* Greenwich, CT: Information Age.

Beane, J. A. (1997). *Curriculum integration: Designing the core of democratic education.* New York: Teachers College Press.

Beane, J. A. (2005). *A reason to teach: Creating classrooms of dignity and hope.* Portsmouth, NH: Heinemann.

Erb, T. O. (Ed.). (2005). *This we believe in action: Implementing successful middle level schools.* Westerville, OH: National Middle School Association.

Jackson, A. W., & Davis, G. A. (2000). *Turning points 2000: Educating adolescents in the 21st century.* New York & Westerville, OH: Teachers College Press & National Middle School Association.

Kaye, C. B. (2004). *The complete guide to service-learning: Proven, practical ways to engage students in civic responsibility, academic curriculum, & social action.* Minneapolis, MN: Free Spirit.

National Research Council. (2005). *How students learn: History, mathematics, and science in the classroom.* Washington, DC: The National Academies Press.

Schultz, B. D. (2008). *Spectacular things happen along the way: Lessons from an urban classroom.* New York: Teachers College Press.

Silver, D. (2005). *Drumming to the beat of different marchers: Finding the rhythm for differentiated learning.* Nashville, TN: Incentive Publications.

Springer, M. (2006). *Soundings: A democratic student-centered education.* Westerville, OH: National Middle School Association.

Stiggins, R., Arter, J. A., Chappuis, J., & Chappuis, S. (2007). *Classroom assessment for student learning: Doing it right-using it well.* New York: Merrill.

Tomlinson, C. A., & McTighe, J. (2006). *Integrating differentiated instruction and understanding by design: Connecting content and kids.* Alexandria, VA: Association for Supervision and Curriculum Development.

Leadership & Organization

Research Summary

Credible research on middle grades leadership and organization documents the importance of a shared vision among the stakeholders—teachers and principals, students and parents, as well as school district personnel and community members. Developed collaboratively, embraced collectively, and used as a lens to guide decision making, vision is a commonly held construct in effective middle schools. Not only does a link exist between a commonly shared vision and the development and maintenance of quality middle schools (George & Anderson, 1989), but there is also convincing evidence that effective middle schools are essential for U.S. educational reform to be successful (Capraro, Capraro, Yetkiner, Rangel-Chavez, & Lewis, 2010). Additionally, parents who are familiar with middle grades practices inherent in the school vision are more likely to have positive attitudes and engagement with the school (Mulhall, Mertens, & Flowers, 2001).

Leadership entails having the tenacity to remain dedicated to the common vision as students and faculty change from year to year. School leadership, commonly considered the administrative team, is not the only leadership that contributes to a successful and productive middle grades organization. In fact, leadership at the teacher level helps to assimilate new teachers, sustain expectations, and promote collaboration and community (Epstein, 1995). To support school and classroom efforts to improve instructional practice, teacher leaders need to be empowered by principals (Zepeda & Mayers, 2002).

School leadership is foundational to ensuring functional and successful middle grades schools (Brown & Anfara, 2002; Clark & Clark, 2008; Thompson, 2004). As a cornerstone of successful schools, leaders need to update continuously their knowledge of exemplary programs and practices. Notably, research findings indicate that effective leadership affects student learning (Leithwood, Louis, Anderson, & Wahlstrom, 2004). As previously mentioned, teachers and other stakeholders play essential roles in developing and sustaining successful schools; however, effective middle school principals are crucial for schools' long-term success. "No single individual is more important to initiating and sustaining improvement in middle grades school students' performance than the school principal" (Jackson & Davis, 2000, p. 157). Effective middle school principals encourage, support, and sustain positive school-wide change based on their knowledge of young adolescent development (Brown & Anfara); curriculum (Brown, Claudet, & Olivarez,

2002); instruction (Marks & Printy, 2003); educational standards (Clark & Clark); and their own professional disposition regarding programs, practices, and trends in middle grades schools (Valentine, 1993; Valentine, Clark, Hackmann, & Petzko, 2004).

Effective middle grades leaders are characterized as courageous and collaborative (Anfara et al., 2003; Anfara et al., 2008; Kinney & Robinson, 2005; NMSA, 2003). Courageous leaders "step outside the box" to help the organization establish suitable goals for their schools; collaborative leaders seek the input and are inclusive of teachers, parents, and other principal stakeholders in school decision making. Effective leaders also facilitate school-district-university partnerships (Goldring & Sims, 2005) and the development of small learning communities (Bishop & Allen-Malley, 2004; George & Lounsbury, 2000; Rottier, Woulf, Bonetti, & Meyer, 2009; Wild, Mayeaux, & Edmonds, 2008) to improve the quality of the teaching and learning processes in their schools.

Middle grades educators deserve continual opportunities for professional development. Recent research confirms that effective professional development is ongoing, connects to instructional practice, centers on student learning and teaching specific content, aligns with school improvement initiatives, and fosters collegial relationships (Darling-Hammond, Wei, Richardson, & Orphanos, 2009; Garet, Porter, Desimone, Birman, & Yoon, 2001; Mertens & Flowers, 2004). Professional learning communities, a forum for professional development, afford teachers a greater sense of ownership of their disciplines and grade groups as well as increased ownership of their curricula. Ultimately, the goal and benefit of effective professional development for teachers is improved student learning (Guskey, 2003).

Organizational structures have potential for fostering positive learning environments for young adolescents. Interdisciplinary teams, a hallmark of the middle school concept, create smaller learning communities where middle grades youth are not lost within the larger school community (Dickinson & Erb, 1997). Evidence links interdisciplinary teams with positive student outcomes—notably, greater student achievement. (Flowers,

Mertens, & Mulhall, 1999; Mertens & Flowers, 2006). Additionally, interdisciplinary teams have a positive effect on middle school students' social bonding (Wallace, 2007). Also, teachers know students more as individuals and are able to share information more effectively with other teachers who teach the same student. Teams—smaller learning communities—give schools greater control over school setting and climate, empower teachers to be proactive and remain highly attuned to students, and promote communication with parents (Cotton, 2001; Supovitz & Christman, 2005). As previously noted, smaller learning communities facilitate the growth of professional learning communities, which offer fertile ground for teachers' ongoing professional development.

> Effective middle school principals are crucial for schools' long-term success.

As schools seek answers to what works for middle schools in terms of leadership and organization, we note the inextricable link between research and practice. School leaders look to research that is relevant to their context; researchers pose research questions to explore practice.

Middle grades leaders and researchers alike can glean insights into effective middle grades leadership and organization through their individual and collective efforts. Central to effective middle grades leadership and organization are (a) establishing a sense of ownership and responsibility for shared and collaborative leadership, (b) building a shared vision among all stakeholders, (c) developing structures to address social and academic challenges unique to middle school youth, and (d) creating a school climate where all stakeholders feel comfortable interacting and discussing important educational issues.

References

Anfara, V. A., Jr., Andrews, P. G., Hough, D. L., Mertens, S. B., Mizelle, N. B., & White, G. P. (2003). *Research and resources in support of This We Believe.* Westerville, OH: National Middle School Association.

Anfara, V. A., Jr. , Pate, P. E., Caskey, M. M., Andrews, G., Daniel, L. G., Mertens, S. B., & Muir, M. (2008). *Research summary: Courageous, collaborative leadership.* Retrieved April 6, 2009, from http://www.nmsa.org/portals/0/pdf/research/Research_Summaries/Courageous_Leadership.pdf

Bishop, P., & Allen-Malley, G. (2004). *The power of two: Partner teams in action.* Westerville, OH: National Middle School Association.

Brown, K. M., & Anfara, V. A., Jr. (2002). *From the desk of the middle school principal.* Lanham, MD: Scarecrow.

Brown, R. S., Claudet, J. G., & Olivarez, A. (2002). Investigating organizational dimensions of middle school curricular leadership: Linkages to school effectiveness. *Research in Middle Level Education Online, 26*(1), 1-13. Retrieved April 1, 2009, from http://www.nmsa.org/portals/0/pdf/publications/RMLE/rmle_vol26_no1_article5.pdf

Capraro, M. M., Capraro, R. M., Yetkiner, Z. E., Rangel-Chavez, A. F., & Lewis, C. W. (2010, In Press). Examining Hispanic students' mathematics performance on high-stakes tests: An examination of one urban school district in Colorado. *Urban Review, 42*(3).

Clark, S. N., & Clark, D. C. (2008). *Leadership that makes a difference: Revitalizing middle schools.* Westerville, OH: National Middle School Association.

Cotton, K. (2001). *New small learning communities: Findings from recent literature.* Portland, OR: Northwest Regional Educational Laboratory. Retrieved August 15, 2009, from http://www3.scasd.org/small_schools/nlsc.pdf

Darling-Hammond, L., Wei, R. C., Andree, A., Richardson, N., & Orphanos, S. (2009). *Professional learning in the learning profession: A status report on teacher development in the United States and abroad.* Dallas, TX: National Staff Development Council.

Dickinson, T. E., & Erb, T. O. (Eds.). (1997). *We gain more than we give: Teaming in middle schools.* Westerville, OH: National Middle School Association.

Epstein, J. L. (1995). School, family, community partnerships: Caring for the children we share. *Phi Delta Kappan, 76,* 701–706.

Flowers, N., Mertens, S., & Mulhall, P. (1999). The impact of teaming: Five research-based outcomes of teaming. *Middle School Journal, 31*(2), 57–60.

Garet, M. S., Porter, A. C., Desimone, L., Birman, B. F., & Yoon, K. S. (2001). What makes professional development effective? Results from a national sample of teachers. *American Educational Research Journal, 38,* 915–945.

George, P. S., & Anderson, W. G. (1989). Maintaining the middle school: A national survey. *NASSP Bulletin, 73*(521), 67–74.

George, P. S., & Lounsbury, J. H. (2000). *Making big schools feel small: Multiage grouping, looping, and schools-within-a-school.* Westerville, OH: National Middle School Association.

Goldring, E., & Sims, P. (2005). Modeling creative and courageous school leadership through district-community-university partnerships. *Educational Policy, 19*(1), 223–249.

Guskey, T. R. (2003). What makes professional development effective? *Phi Delta Kappan, 84,* 748–750.

Jackson, A. W., & Davis, G. A. (2000). *Turning points 2000: Educating adolescents in the 21st century.* New York & Westerville, OH: Teachers College Press & National Middle School Association.

Kinney, P., & Robinson, L. (2005). Courageous, collaborative leadership. In T. O. Erb (Ed.), *This we believe in action: Implementing successful middle level schools* (pp. 19–27).Westerville, OH: National Middle School Association.

Leithwood, K., Louis, K. S., Anderson, S., & Wahlstrom, K. (2004). *How leadership influences student learning. Review of research.* New York: The Wallace Foundation.

Marks, H. M., & Printy, S. M. (2003). Principal leadership and school performance: An integration of transformational and instructional leadership. *Educational Administration Quarterly, 39,* 370–397.

Mertens, S. B., & Flowers, N. (2004). *Research summary: Professional development for teachers.* Retrieved April 7, 2009, from http://www.nmsa.org/portals/0/pdf/research/Research_Summaries/Professional_Development.pdf

Mertens, S. B., & Flowers, N. (2006). Middle Start's impact on comprehensive middle school reform. *Middle Grades Research Journal, 1*(1), 1–26.

Mulhall, P. F., Mertens, S. B., & Flowers, N. (2001). How familiar are parents with middle level practices? *Middle School Journal, 33*(2), 57–61.

National Middle School Association. (2003). *This we believe: Successful schools for young adolescents.* Westerville, OH: Author.

Rottier, J., Woulf, T., Bonetti, D., & Meyer, E. (2009). *Teaming & advisory: Perfect partners.* Westerville, OH: National Middle School Association.

Supovitz, J. A., & Christman, J. B. (2005). Small learning communities that actually learn: Lessons for school leaders, *Phi Delta Kappan, 86,* 649-652.

Thompson, S. C. (Ed.). (2004). *Reforming middle level education: Considerations for policy makers.* Greenwich, CT: Information Age.

Valentine, J. W. (1993). *Leadership in middle level education: A national survey of middle level leaders and schools.* Reston, VA: National Association of Secondary School Principals.

Valentine, J. W., Clark, D., Hackmann, D., & Petzko, V. (2004). *A national study of leadership in middle level schools: Volume II: Leadership for highly successful middle level schools.* Reston, VA: National Association of Secondary School Principals.

Wallace, J. J. (2007). Effects of interdisciplinary teaching team configuration upon the social bonding of middle school students. *Research in Middle Level Education Online, 30*(5), 1–18. Retrieved July 25, 2009, from http://www.nmsa.org/portals/0/pdf/publications/RMLE/rmle_vol30_no5.pdf

Wild, M. D., Mayeaux, A. S., & Edmonds, K. P. (2008). *Teamwork: Setting the standard for collaborative teaching, grades 5–9.* Westerville, OH: National Middle School Association.

Zepeda, S. J., & Mayers, R. S. (2002). A case study of leadership in the middle grades: The work of the instructional lead teacher. *Research in Middle Level Education Online, 25*(1), 1–11. Retrieved April 1, 2009, from http://www.nmsa.org/portals/0/pdf/publications/RMLE/rmle_vol25_no1_article1.pdf

Leadership & Organization Characteristics

A shared vision developed by all stakeholders guides every decision. (Shared Vision)

Annotated References

George, P. S., & Anderson, W. G. (1989). Maintaining the middle school: A national survey. *NASSP Bulletin, 73*(521), 67-74.

George and Anderson identified a link between a clear and shared vision and the creation and maintenance of high-quality middle school programs. To explore ways to maintain an effective middle school, they surveyed administrators (*n* = 98) from the nations reputedly successful middle schools who had participated in an earlier national study (George & Oldaker, 1985). George and Anderson concluded, "Understanding the purpose of the middle school, and the school's commitment to the personal and educational needs of young adolescents appears to play a most important role, both prior to and following the implementation of quality middle schools" (p. 69).

George, P. S., & Oldaker, L. L. (1985). *Evidence for the middle school.* Columbus, OH: National Middle School Association.

Mulhall, P. F., Mertens, S. B., & Flowers, N. (2001). How familiar are parents with middle level practices? *Middle School Journal, 33*(2), 57–61.

In this article, Mulhall, Mertens, and Flowers focused on parent familiarity with specific middle grades practices (i.e., advisory programs, cooperative learning, exploratory activities, heterogeneous grouping, integrated lessons, interdisciplinary teaming). As part of their ongoing evaluation of middle grades reform using the School Improvement Self-Study (conducted by the Center for Prevention Research and Development at the University of Illinois), the research team analyzed parent survey data from 131 schools in Arkansas, Louisiana, and Mississippi. Findings revealed that parents were not generally aware of middle school programs and practices; however, Mulhall and colleagues reported, "Parents reporting high familiarity with middle level practices were more likely to report positive attitudes and engagement at their child's school" (p. 60).

Leaders are committed to and knowledgeable about this age group, educational research, and best practices. (Committed Leaders)

Annotated References

Brown, R. S., Claudet, J. G., & Olivarez, A. (2002). Investigating organizational dimensions of middle school curricular leadership: Linkages to school effectiveness. *Research in Middle Level Education Online, 26*(1), 1-13. Retrieved April 1, 2009, from http://www.nmsa.org/portals/0/pdf/publications/RMLE/rmle_vol26_no1_article5.pdf

Brown, Claudet, and Olivarez explored the organizational structure of curricular leadership in middle school settings. Using the Organization Curricular Leadership Inventory (OCLI) as a survey instrument, these researchers determined that curricular leadership involves an interactive activity across a number of educational roles. They found that the OCLI provides an appropriate tool for judging a leadership environment.

Marks, H. M., & Printy, S. M. (2003). Principal leadership and school performance: An integration of transformational and instructional leadership. *Educational Administration Quarterly, 39,* 370–397.

In their study, Marks and Printy examined the collaboration of teachers and principals and the potential of this collaboration to affect teaching and student achievement. Participants included 24 nationally selected restructured schools (8 elementary, 8 middle, and 8 high schools). Using hierarchical linear modeling, the authors determined that transformational leadership is a necessary but insufficient condition for instructional leadership. They reported, "When transformational and shared instructional leadership coexist in an integrated form of leadership, the influence on school performance, measured by the quality of its pedagogy and the achievement of its students, is substantial" (p. 370).

Valentine, J. W. (1993). *Leadership in middle level education: A national survey of middle level leaders and schools.* Reston, VA: National Association of Secondary School Principals.

In this volume, Valentine shared the roles and professional beliefs of middle grades school principals, assistant principals, and leadership team members. Data came from a national survey distributed to 2,000 middle grades schools. The survey targeted personal characteristics, job roles and tasks, and professional beliefs as well as the programs, practices, and trends in middle grades schools. Valentine reported the results related to personal and professional characteristics, school leadership, educational programs, issues and trends, and leadership profiles.

Zepeda, S. J., & Mayers, R. S. (2002). A case study of leadership in the middle grades: The work of the instructional lead teacher. *Research in Middle Level Education Online, 25*(1), 1-11. Retrieved April 1, 2009, from http://www.nmsa.org/portals/0/pdf/publications/RMLE/rmle_vol25_no1_article1.pdf

In this research article, Zepeda and Mayers described their qualitative study of middle grades leadership. Using case study methodology, they examined the work of one middle grades instructional lead teacher and documented his efforts toward becoming an instructional leader. They reported the tensions caused by assigning the lead teacher administrative duties, which impeded his work as an instructional leader. They found that the goal of instructional leadership should remain focused on supporting teachers' efforts to improve instructional practice.

Leaders demonstrate courage and collaboration.

(Courageous & Collaborative Leaders)

Annotated References

Anfara, V. A., Jr., Pate, P. E., Caskey, M. M., Andrews, G., Daniel, L. G., Mertens, S. B., & Muir, M. (2008). *Research summary: Courageous, collaborative leadership.* Retrieved April 6, 2009, from http://www.nmsa.org/portals/0/pdf/research/Research_Summaries/Courageous_Leadership.pdf

In this research summary, Anfara and colleagues (2008) identified common elements of leadership: (a) helping organizations to establish appropriate and defensible goals, and (b) influencing members to accomplish these goals. They defined courageous leadership as the ability to "step outside the box and take chances" to help the school establish appropriate and defensible goals and collaborative leadership as the ability to include all stakeholders in decision making. They noted that these leaders along with their teams have a vision that enables them to act ethically when making decisions for the greater good of the organization. Anfara and colleagues asserted that effective leadership is "fundamentally about developing people, setting directions, and redesigning the organization." Their summary also articulated implications for courageous, collaborative leadership in middle grades schools as well as a list of recommended resources.

> Courageous leadership is defined as the ability to "step outside the box and take chances."

Goldring, E., & Sims, P. (2005). Modeling creative and courageous school leadership through district-community-university partnerships. *Educational Policy, 19*(1), 223–249.

Goldring and Sims detailed their qualitative study of the Principals Leadership Academy of Nashville (PLAN) and the development of successful university-community-district partnerships. They conducted interviews (n = 14) with principal stakeholders including the superintendent of schools, the dean of the college of education, the president and executive director of the Public Education Foundation, the education coordinator of a local Rotary Club, members of the curriculum design team, and academy leaders. Analyses indicated that interorganizational partnerships thrived when (a) grounded in shared power and shared learning, and (b) top-level leaders were highly visible and champions of the partnership.

Leithwood, K., Louis, K. S., Anderson, S., & Wahlstrom, K. (2004). *How leadership influences student learning. Review of research.* New York: The Wallace Foundation.

In their comprehensive review of research, Leithwood, Louis, Anderson, and Wahlstrom examined the existing evidence on school leadership. They developed and used a framework that features 10 interdependent variables to serve as an organizer for the review of the research literature. Using the framework, they explored how leadership affects student learning. They reported that (a) school leadership was second only to teaching among school-related factors that influence student learning, and (b) the effects of successful school leadership were greater in schools with the most need. In addition to documenting how leadership promotes student achievement, the researchers summarized the basics of successful leadership, and offered specific recommendations (i.e., set a clear vision, support and develop talented staff, build a solid organizational structure) for educational leaders.

Valentine, J. W., Clark, D., Hackmann, D., & Petzko, V. (2004). *A national study of leadership in middle level schools: Volume II: Leadership for highly successful middle level schools.* Reston, VA: National Association of Secondary School Principals.

In this volume, Valentine, Clark, Hackmann, and Petzko reported the findings from a National Association of Secondary School Principals' decade study of middle grades leadership—the National Study of Leadership in Middle Level

Schools. They documented lessons learned from the collection of survey data from principals, teachers, students, and parents in 98 middle grades schools. Using data collected at six selected school sites, they developed detailed profiles of these highly successful middle grades principals and their schools. Valentine and colleagues described personal leadership qualities, leadership for change, leadership for teaching and learning, and leadership for resource management. They also identified specific behaviors of effective middle grades leaders.

Ongoing professional development reflects best educational practices. (Professional Development)

Annotated References

Darling-Hammond, L., Wei, R. C., Andree, A., Richardson, N., & Orphanos, S. (2009). *Professional learning in the learning profession: A status report on teacher development in the United States and abroad.* Dallas, TX: National Staff Development Council.

In this comprehensive report, Darling-Hammond, Wei, Andree, Richardson, and Orphanos synthesized the research base on professional learning and teacher development. The authors organized their findings in three chapters: (1) Effective Professional Development: What Does the Research Show? (2) Professional Development Abroad: Trends and Strategies, and (3) The Status of Professional Development in the U.S. Their analyses regarding the research on professional development, showed that effective professional development (a) is intensive, ongoing, and connected to practice; (b) focuses on student learning and address the teaching of specific content; (c) aligns with school improvement priorities and goals; and (d) builds strong working relationships among teachers. Analyses of recent data (i.e., 2003-04 Schools and Staffing Survey, 2004–05 MetLife Survey, and 2007-08 National Staff Development Council Standards Assessment Inventory) indicated increased availability of induction and mentoring programs and improvement in building teachers' content knowledge; however, additional structures and supports are needed to sustain teacher learning and to provide job-embedded professional development in collegial environments.

Garet, M. S., Porter, A. C., Desimone, L., Birman, B. F., & Yoon, K. S. (2001). What makes professional development effective? Results from a national sample of teachers. *American Educational Research Journal, 38,* 915–945.

In this large-scale empirical study, Garet, Porter, Desimone, Birman, and Yoon examined the effects of professional development on teachers' learning. They surveyed a nationally representative sample of 1,027 mathematics and science teachers who had participated in professional development activities (i.e., Eisenhower Professional Development Program). Analyses of survey data revealed three core features of professional development activities have significant positive effects on teachers' self-reported increase in knowledge and skills as well as changes in classroom practice: (a) focus on content knowledge, (b) opportunities for active learning, and (c) coherence with other learning activities. The authors found that three core, structural features significantly affected learning: (1) the form of the activity; (2) collective participation of teachers from the same school, grade, or discipline; and (3) the duration of the activity.

Mertens, S. B., & Flowers, N. (2004). *Research summary: Professional development for teachers.* Retrieved April 7, 2009, from http://www.nmsa.org/portals/0/pdf/research/Research_Summaries/Professional_Development.pdf

In this research summary, Mertens and Flowers described professional development as a wide range of formal and informal processes and activities that teachers engage in to improve their practice—both inside and outside the school. After indicating that the best way to improve teacher effectiveness is through regular, high-quality professional development, they cited the research that documents how professional development links to student achievement. The authors also identified the benefits (e.g., improved student learning) and characteristics (e.g., based on research evidence) of high–quality professional development as well as provided examples of both formal (e.g., attending workshops or conferences) and informal (e.g., regular collaboration in teams) professional development experiences.

Organizational structures foster purposeful learning and meaningful relationships. (Organizational Structures)

Annotated References

Daniel, L. (2007). *Research summary: Multiage grouping.* Retrieved April 3, 2009, from http://www.nmsa.org/portals/0/pdf/research/Research_Summaries/Multiage_Grouping.pdf

In this research summary, Daniel defined multiage grouping in relation to both learning and relationship building. He noted the overall scarcity of research on the practice and explained the findings that exist have "either favored multiage grouping or yielded no statistically significant differences between outcomes of students and teachers in multiage and single-grade classes" (p. 2). Positive outcomes have included enhanced self-concept, increased social bonding, fewer discipline referrals, and positive attitudes toward school. Daniel also considered the overall findings related to student achievement thus far to be inconclusive but verified sufficient evidence for affective advantages of multiage grouping.

Flowers, N., Mertens, S., & Mulhall, P. (1999). The impact of teaming: Five research-based outcomes of teaming. *Middle School Journal, 31*(2), 57–60.

In this article, Flowers, Mertens, and Mulhall described five research-based outcomes of interdisciplinary teaching. Their analyses of survey data collected from 155 middle grades schools in Michigan that had participated in the School Improvement Self-Study (conducted by the center for Prevention Research and Development at the University of Illinois) showed the significant effects of teaming. They found five empirically based outcomes: (1) common planning is a critical component of teaming; (2) teaming improves work climate; (3) teaming increases parent contacts; (4) teaming increases teachers' job satisfaction; and (5) teaming is associated with higher student achievement.

George, P. S., & Lounsbury, J. H. (2000). *Making big schools feel small: Multiage grouping, looping, and schools-within-a-school.* Westerville, OH: National Middle School Association.

In their definitive book, George and Lounsbury described three alternative structures (i.e., multiage grouping, looping, schools-within-a-school) for organizing middle grades students for instruction to maximize relationships among faculty and students. In addition to detailed explanation of these structures, they provided examples of successful implementation and discussed how multiage grouping can be used for non-instructional activities (e.g., advisory). George and Lounsbury included a review of research to document the effects of these structures on the academic and social success of young adolescents as well as a summary of their own national survey of schools implementing structures to build long-term relationships with students. They also provided a set of guidelines for implementing multiage grouping and other similar structures.

Mertens, S. B., & Flowers, N. (2004). *Research summary: Interdisciplinary teaming.* Retrieved April 3, 2009, from http://www.nmsa.org/portals/0/pdf/research/Research_Summaries/Interdisciplinary_Teaming.pdf

This research summary defined interdisciplinary teaming and included key principles for organizing effective teams and essential characteristics of highly effective teams. Mertens and Flowers highlighted research on this cornerstone practice of middle schools, identifying several positive student outcomes—academic and affective alike—when teaming is implemented effectively. In particular, they noted the importance of common planning time as crucial to a team's success.

Roney, K., Anfara, V. A., Jr., & Brown, K. M. (2008). *Creating organizationally healthy and effective middle schools: Research that supports the middle school concept and student achievement.* Westerville, OH: National Middle School Association.

In this volume, Roney, Anfara, and Brown provided an in-depth exploration of organizational health and middle schools. After presenting an overview of the middle school concept, the authors articulated the influence of organizational health in middle grades education. Next, they provided four case studies that document the relationship among middle school reform initiatives, organization health, and student achievement. Roney and colleagues also included reflections from seven practitioners to illustrate these connections and serve as a bridge between research and practice. In the final section of the book, they synthesized the effective schools research and offered specific actions for middle grades schools.

Wallace, J. J. (2007). Effects of interdisciplinary teaching team configuration upon the social bonding of middle school students. *Research in Middle Level Education Online, 30*(5), 1-18. Retrieved July 25, 2009, from http://www.nmsa.org/portals/0/pdf/publications/RMLE/rmle_vol30_no5.pdf

This quantitative study measured students' perceived levels of social bonding with their peers, school, and teachers. Examining a sample of 10 teaching teams, the research findings showed students' social bonding to be significantly higher on the smaller two-teacher team than on the traditional four-teacher team configuration. While this study has implications for policy and practice given that four-teacher teams are a common structure in middle schools, Wallace cautioned against over-interpretation. He stressed the importance of teacher role within the team in relation to student outcomes.

Recommended Resources

Andrews, P. G., & Anfara, V. A., Jr. (2003). *Leaders for a movement: Professional preparation and development of middle level teachers and administrators.* Greenwich, CT: Information Age.

Anfara, V. A., Jr., Roney, K., Smarkola, C., DuCette, J. P., & Gross, S. J. (2006). *The developmentally responsive middle level principal: A leadership model and measurement instrument.* Westerville, OH: National Middle School Association.

Bishop, P., & Allen-Malley, G. (2004). *The power of two: Partner teams in action.* Westerville, OH: National Middle School Association.

Brown, K. M., & Anfara, V. A., Jr. (2002). *From the desk of the middle school principal.* Lanham, MD: Scarecrow.

Clark, S. N., & Clark, D. C. (2008). *Leadership that makes a difference: Revitalizing middle schools.* Westerville, OH: National Middle School Association.

Dickinson, T. E., & Erb, T. O. (Eds.). (1997). *We gain more than we give: Teaming in middle schools.* Westerville, OH: National Middle School Association

Epstein, J. L., Sanders, M. G., Simon, B. S., Salinas, K. C., Jansorn, N. R., & Van Voorhis, F. L. (2002). *School, community, and community partnerships: Your handbook for action* (2nd ed.). Thousand Oaks, CA: Corwin.

Flowers, N., Mertens, S. B., Mulhall, P. F., with Krawczyk, T. (2007). *Applying current middle grades research to improve classrooms and schools.* Westerville, OH: National Middle School Association.

Fullan, M. (2003). *The moral imperative of school leadership.* Thousand Oaks, CA: Corwin.

George, P. S., & Lounsbury, J. H. (2000). *Making big schools feel small: Multiage grouping, looping, and schools-within-a-school.* Westerville, OH: National Middle School Association.

Roney, K., Anfara, V. A., Jr., & Brown, K. M. (2008). *Creating organizationally healthy and effective middle schools: Research that supports the middle school concept and student achievement.* Westerville, OH: National Middle School Association.

Rottier, J., Woulf, T., Bonetti, D., & Meyer, E. (2009). *Teaming & advisory: Perfect partners.* Westerville, OH: National Middle School Association.

Thompson, S. C. (Ed.). (2004). *Reforming middle level education: Considerations for policy makers.* Greenwich, CT: Information Age.

Wild, M. D., Mayeaux, A. S., & Edmonds, K. P. (2008). *Teamwork: Setting the standard for collaborative teaching, grades 5–9.* Portland, ME: Stenhouse.

Culture & Community

Research Summary

Using research to guide middle grades education, should positively impact students' achievement and the quality of their lives. However, classroom events and teachers' actions "do not occur without the wider influence of things beyond the classroom walls and beyond the teacher's direct control" (Roe, 2008, p. 11). An attention to culture and community sends a hefty reminder that quality middle grades education programs demand a much broader attention than the traditional focus on cognitive domains and teachers' action.

One reason to focus on dimensions of culture and community is that adolescence is characterized by increasing complexity in both academic and social structure (e.g., Kinney, 1993; Seidman, Aber, Allen, & Sabine, 1996; Simmons & Blyth, 1987), an increase in the number of relationships with peers outside the supervisory scope of the family, the development of dating and romantic relationships, and a decrease of activities within the family (Fletcher, Darling, Steinberg, & Dornsbusch, 1995; Giordano, 2003; Harris, 1998). Adolescents increasingly shift from their family to peers as a primary source for support and interaction. The composition of adolescents' peer groups also changes. Specifically, young adolescents social groups are increasingly similar with respect to their own race and gender (Hartup & Stevens, 1997), their attitudes toward school, and their achievement levels (Berndt & Keefe, 1995; Ryan, 2001). These facts can reinforce and shape adolescent opinions about school and its importance.

> School engagement can improve academic achievement and reduce student disaffection and dropout rates more than a focus on standards.

Second, the National Research Council and Institute of Medicine (2004) drew attention to how school engagement can improve academic achievement and reduce student disaffection and dropout rates more than a focus on standards. In fact, some scholars have argued that the focus on standards further alienates low-performing students, rather than motivating them to increase their performance (e.g., Sheldon & Biddle, 1998). All of these factors are affected by the individuals involved and by the larger structures that shape the formation or growth of peer relationships.

Looking across these basic premises and turning to the research that examines effective culture and community, the importance of several specific areas arise: school climate (or academic press), parent involvement, students' identity and sense of belonging, and peer relationships.

School Climate/Academic Press

Academic press or school climate describes the ways that peer groups' different values affect the larger school environment (Becker, Hughes, & Greer, 1995; Brown, 1990). If the peer groups value their academic education as well as their social education, this value can positively influence a broad range of students, from athletes to those more marginalized. This positive influence results from the culture created in the school as a whole. Such a culture demands the support of students and the professionals involved in the structuring and culturing of the school.

Becker and colleagues (1995), alternatively, suggested that such a large-scale academic climate may not penetrate the tighter knit atmosphere of peer groups. They noted the same kind of mechanism in school as in university settings. Specifically, while the administration and faculty of a university impose similar, if not identical, standards upon students, the students respond quite differently to them. Some students invest heavily in academic matters. Others give proportionately larger emphasis to social aspects. Many of these responses may come from the peer group or social network that supports the student in his or her pursuits.

Young adolescents, however, generally do better in schools that offer a supportive environment, hold students to high academic standards, and have an efficient organization with well-trained teachers and involved parents

(Cook, Herman, Phillips, & Settersten, 2002). Contextual characteristics of schools have also been linked to individual behaviors and experiences in school. Research on the effects of the school environment has shown that a number of student outcomes vary by characteristics of the school such as its grade-span, racial composition, and socioeconomic status (Brooks-Gunn, Duncan, Klebanov, & Sealand, 1993; Bryant, Schulenberg, O'Malley, Bachman, & Johnston, 2003; Teitler & Weiss, 2000).

Academics and researchers have also unveiled a significant relationship between school quality (e.g., principal leadership and school climate) and student success (Gaziel, 1995; Heck, 2000; Irvine, 1988; Leithwood & Montgomery, 1982). Berger and Luckman (1966) stipulated that the organization of the school's formal and informal processes can affect the construction of relationships and the culture of the school. Hord (1997) and other professional community scholars noted the importance of collegial environments in which faculty and staff are supported and support one another in both learning, reflection, and innovation (Astuto, Clark, Read, McGree, & Fernandez, 1994). The creation of cultures such as this for both the adults and the students significantly affects the larger culture of a school as well as the structure and culture of adolescent peer groups. This structural osmosis, therefore, allows school climate, or an academic press, to affect the very identity of young adolescents.

Parent Involvement

Research and common sense concur that parental involvement can be pivotal for middle grades students and their academic achievement. According to Mo and Singh (2008), parents' relationship and involvement significantly affect students' academic success. In a meta-analysis, Fan and Chen (2001) also found significant effects for parents' relationship and involvement on students' academic success. Parents' aspiration or expectation for their children's educational achievement had the strongest relationship to student achievement. As Snow, Porche, Tabrs, and Harris (2007) concluded, "Students with strong support from home and who were well regarded by their teachers were more likely to be progressing well in school, even with only average academic skills" (p. 110).

Students' Identity and Sense of Belonging

According to Anderman (2002), students' sense of school belonging relates positively with optimism, self-concept, and grade point average. These positive outcomes, like others that we explore, hold the possibility for directly or indirectly impacting student achievement.

Young adolescents develop their identity in part by evaluating themselves in various contexts such as social relationships, academics, and extracurricular participation (Masten et al., 1995). Schools are a key site for this evaluation. From a developmental perspective, the middle grades are generally a time of growing concern for popularity, with students placing increasing importance on interpersonal relationships. This shift in emphasis often results in increasingly nonconforming peer values, social competition, and mean behavior (Seidman et al., 1994). Moreover, adults in the school do not have as much of an opportunity as elementary teachers to know what goes on among students, as instruction is structured such that students move from classroom to classroom, limiting student-teacher interaction (Wilson & Herriot, 1989). Similarly, students spend more time outside the school day without supervision than in the elementary grades, which means that adult intervention in the social arena is scarce (Merten, 1997). Participation in extracurricular activities also plays an important role in adolescent self-evaluation (Brown & Lohr, 1987; Larkin, 1979). Because these activities tend to be separate from the academic work of a school, they provide an additional or alternative outlet for students to form their identity (Coleman & Hoffer, 1987; Quiroz, Gonzales, & Frank, 1996). Connections developed through participation in extracurricular activities serve as a significant source of attachment for students, both as a means of identifying with the school and as means of peer identification outside of classroom work (Eder & Parker, 1987; Holland & Andre, 1987; Powell, Farrar, & Cohen, 1985). Extracurricular participation also offers students a forum in which

> This shift in emphasis often results in increasingly nonconforming peer values, social competition, and mean behavior.

to demonstrate skill and accomplishment in a setting that may not require academic accomplishment (Eccles & Barber, 1999; Larson, 2000).

Peer Relationships

This research summary on community and culture ends with peer relationships, in part, because of their overarching influence. Recall that peer relationships appeared in the section on school climate. Then, peer relationships also impacted students' identify and sense of belonging. However, peer relationships hold empirical support that attests to their stand-alone importance. For example, using a self-report questionnaire, Nelson and DeBacker (2008) determined the variance in achievement motivation explained by peer relationships. Specifically, adolescents who felt valued and respected by their peers reported higher levels of achievement motivation. To affect achievement, however, students' peer reference groups must also have an academic orientation (Harter, 1993; Harter & Connell, 1984).

As evidenced by the aforementioned research, culture and community components warrant equal footing with areas that traditionally receive greater attention. Jackson and Davis (2000) reported, "What happens to young people within their families, neighborhoods, peer groups, religious institutions, out-of-school programs and a wide range of other formal and informal relationships and settings can easily have as much or more impact on how young people 'turn out' as the middle grades school" (p. 209). Simply stated, culture and community matter.

References

Anderman, E. M. (2002). School effects on psychological outcomes during adolescence. *Journal of Learning Disabilities, 31*(2), 128–138.

Astuto, T. A., Clark, D. L., Read, A., McGree, K., & Fernandez, L. D. K. P. (1994). *Roots of reform: Challenging the assumptions that control change in education.* Bloomington, IN: Phi Delta Kappa Educational Foundation.

Becker, H., Hughes, S. E. C., & Geer, B. (1995). *Making the grade: The academic side of college life.* New York: Wiley.

Berger, P. L., & Luckman, T. (1966). *The social construction of knowledge.* New York: Doubleday.

Berndt, T. J., & Keefe, K. (1995). Friends' influence on adolescents' adjustment to school. *Child Development, 66,* 1312-1329.

Brooks-Gunn, J., Duncan, G. J., Klebanov, P., & Sealand, N. (1993). Do neighborhoods influence child and adolescent development? *American Journal of Sociology, 102,* 353-395.

Brown, B. B. (1990). Peer groups and peer cultures. In S. S. Feldman & G. R. Elliott (Eds.), *At the threshold: The developing adolescent* (pp. 171-196). Boston: Harvard University Press.

Brown, B. B., & Lohr, M. J. (1987). Peer-group affiliation and adolescent self-esteem: An integration of ego-identity and symbolic interaction theories. *Journal of Personality and Social Psychology, 43,* 18–29.

Bryant, A. L., Schulenberg, J. E., O'Malley, P. M., Bachman, J. G., & Johnston, L. D. (2003). How academic achievement, attitudes, and behaviors relate to the course of substance use during adolescence: A 6-year multiwave national longitudinal study. *Journal of Research on Adolescence, 13,* 361–397.

Coleman, J. S., & Hoffer, T. (1987). *Public and private high schools: The impact of communities.* New York: Basic Books.

Cook, T. D., Herman, M. R., Phillips, M., & Settersten, R. A. (2002). Some ways in which neighborhoods, nuclear families, friendship groups, and schools jointly affect changes in early adolescent development. *Child Development, 73*(4), 1283–1309.

Eccles, J. S., & Barber, B. L. (1999). Student council, volunteering, basketball, or marching band: What kinds of extracurricular involvement matters? *Journal of Adolescent Research, 14,* 10–43.

Eder, D., & Parker, S. (1987). The cultural reproduction of gender: The effect of extracurricular activities on peer-group culture. *Sociology of Education, 60,* 200–213.

Fan, X., & Chen, M. (2001). Parental involvement and students = academic achievement: A meta-analysis. *Educational Psychology Review, 13*(1), 1–22.

Fletcher, A. C., Darling, N. E., Steinberg, L., & Dornbusch, S. M. (1995). The company they keep: Relation of adolescents' adjustment and behavior to their friends' perception of authoritative parenting in the social network. *Developmental Psychology, 31*, 300–310.

Gaziel, H. (1995). Managerial work patterns of principals at high- and low-performing Israeli elementary schools. *The Elementary School Journal, 96*(2), 179–194.

Giordano, P. C. (2003). Relationships in adolescence. *Annual Review of Sociology, 29*, 257–281.

Harris, J. R. (1998). *The nurture assumption: Why children turn out the way they do.* New York: Free Press.

Harter, S. (1993). Causes and consequences of low self-esteem in children and adolescents. In R. F. Baumeister (Ed.), *Self-esteem: The puzzle of low self-regard* (pp. 87–116). New York: Kluwer Academic/Plenum.

Harter, S., & Connell, J. P. (1984). A model of children's achievement and related self-perceptions of competence, control and motivational orientation. In J. Nicholls (Ed.), *Advances in motivation and achievement* (pp. 219–250). Greenwich, CT: JAI Press.

Hartup, W., & Stevens, N. (1997). Friendship and adaptation in the life course. *Psychological Bulletin, 121*, 355–370.

Heck, R. (2000). Examining the impact of school quality on school outcomes and improvement: A value-added approach. *Educational Administration Quarterly, 36*, 513–552.

Holland, A., & Andre, T. (1987). Participation in extracurricular activities in secondary school: What is known, what needs to be known. *Review of Educational Research, 57*, 437–466.

Hord, S. M. (1997). *Professional learning communities: Communities of continuous inquiry and improvement.* Austin, TX: Southwest Educational Development Laboratory.

Irvine, J. J. (1988). Urban schools that work: A summary of relevant factors. *Journal of Negro Education, 57*(3), 238–242.

Jackson, A. W., & Davis, G. A. (2000). *Turning points 2000: Educating adolescents in the 21ˢᵗ century.* New York & Westerville, OH: Teachers College Press & National Middle School Association.

Kinney, D. A. (1993). From nerds to normals: The recovery of identity among adolescents from middle school to high school. *Sociology of Education, 66,* 21–40.

Larkin, R. W. (1979). *Suburban youth in cultural crisis.* New York: Oxford University Press.

Larson, R. W. (2000). Toward a psychology of positive youth development. *American Psychologist, 55,* 170–183.

Leithwood, K. A., & Montgomery, D. J. (1982). The role of the elementary school principal in program improvement. *Review of Educational Research, 52,* 309–339.

Masten, A., Coatsworth, J., Neemann, J., Gest, S., Tellege, A., & Garmezy, N. (1995). The structure and coherence of competence from childhood through adolescence. *Child Development, 66,* 1635–1659.

Merten, D. E. (1997). The meaning of meanness: Popularity, competition, and conflict among junior high school girls. *Sociology of Education, 70,* 175–191.

Mo, Y., & Singh, K. (2008). Parents' relationships and involvement: Effects on students' engagement and performance. *Research in Middle Level Education Online, 31*(10), 1–11. Retrieved July 25, 2009, from http://www.nmsa.org/portals/0/pdf/publications/RMLE/rmle_vol31_no10.pdf

National Research Council and the Institute of Medicine. (2004). *Engaging schools: Fostering high school students' motivation to learn.* Committee on increasing high school students' engagement and motivation to learn. Washington, DC: The National Academies Press.

Nelson, R. M., & DeBacker, T. K. (2008). Achievement motivation in adolescents: The role of peer climate and best friends. *Journal of Experimental Education, 76*(2), 170–189.

Powell, A. G., Farrar, E., & Cohen, D. K. (1985). *The shopping mall high school: Winners and losers in the educational marketplace.* Boston: Houghton Mifflin.

Quiroz, P. A., Gonzalez, N. F., & Frank, K. A. (1996). Carving a niche in the high school social structure: Formal and informal constraints on participation in the extra curriculum. *Research in Sociology of Education and Socialization, 11,* 93–120.

Roe, M. F. (2008, December). *The ways teachers do the things they do: Differentiation in middle level literacy classes.* Paper presented at the annual meeting of the National Reading Conference. Orlando, FL.

Ryan, A. M. (2001). The peer group as a context for the development of young adolescent motivation and achievement. *Child Development, 72,* 1135–1150.

Seidman, E., Aber, L. J., Allen, L., & Sabine, E. F. (1996). The impact of the transition to high school on the self-system and perceived social context of poor urban youth. *American Journal of Community Psychology, 24,* 489–515.

Sheldon K., & Biddle, B. (1998). Standards, accountability, and school reform: Perils and pitfalls. *Teachers College Record, 100,* 164–180.

Simmons, R. G., & Blyth, D. A. (1987). *Moving into adolescence: The impact of pubertal change and school context.* New York: DeGruyter.

Snow, C. E., Porche, M. V., Tabors, P. O., & Harris, S. R. (2007). *Is literacy enough: Pathways to academic success for adolescents.* Baltimore, MD: Brookes.

Teitler, J. O., & Weiss, C. C. (2000). Effects of neighborhood and school environments on transitions to first sexual intercourse. *Sociology of Education, 73,* 112–132.

Wilson, B. L., & Herriot, R. E. (1989). *Formal subunits within American public schools: Their structure, power, and consequences.* Philadelphia: Research for Better Schools.

Culture & Community Characteristics

The school environment is inviting, safe, inclusive, and supportive of all. (School Environment)

Annotated References

Jackson, A. W., & Davis, G. A. (2000). *Turning points 2000: Educating adolescents in the 21st century.* New York & Westerville, OH: Teachers College Press & National Middle School Association.

In this volume, Jackson and Davis provided a "comprehensive and comprehensible model" for educating young adolescents. They described efforts to implement the recommendations from *Turning Points: Preparing American Youth for the 21st Century* (Carnegie Council on Adolescent Development, 1989) and other policy initiatives. They also noted middle grades improvement efforts and research about the schooling of young adolescents. The authors centered their model on an overall goal—ensuring success for every student. Notably, Jackson and Davis included as one of their seven recommendations, "Provide a safe and healthy school environment as part of improving academic performance and developing caring and ethical citizens" (p. 24).

> Carnegie Council on Adolescent Development. (1989). *Turning points: Preparing American youth for the 21st century.* New York: Carnegie Corporation.

Morocco, C. C., Clark-Chiarelli, N., Aguilar, C. M., & Brigham, N. (2002). Cultures of excellence and belonging in urban middle schools. *Research in Middle Level Education Online, 25*(2), 1-15. Retrieved July 25, 2009, from http://www.nmsa.org/portals/0/pdf/publications/RMLE/rmle_vol25_no2_article4.pdf

Based on a qualitative investigation across a three-year period, Morocco, Clark-Chiarelli, Aguilar, and Brigham (2002) determined seven features that define a high-performing culture that accommodates a range of students. First, they noted the need for a philosophical system that believes in all students' achievement, commits to a collaborative learning environment, and supports students' development as lifelong learners. Second, they specified the need for administrators and school leaders who can respond to challenging situations when they arise. In addition, they unveiled the importance of collaborative organizational structures such as teaming and grouping. They also highlighted the importance of coherent and consistent instructional practices that students experience across classrooms and articulated understandings of the definition of a learner, and a consistent discourse about student learning. Their final feature asserted the centrality of partnerships between parents, community, and school personnel.

Nelson, R. M., & DeBacker, T. K. (2008). Achievement motivation in adolescents: The role of peer climate and best friends. *Journal of Experimental Education, 76*(2), 170–189.

Based upon a self-report questionnaire, Nelson and DeBacker determined the variance in achievement motivation could be explained by peer relationships. Specifically, they found that adolescents who felt valued and respected by their peers reported higher levels of achievement motivation.

Every student's academic and personal development is guided by an adult advocate. (Adult Advocate)

Annotated References

Anfara, V. A., Jr. (2006). *Research summary: Advisory programs.* Retrieved July 25, 2009, from http://www.nmsa.org/portals/0/pdf/research/Research_Summaries/Advisory_Programs.pdf

This research summary defined the concept of advisory programs while noting advisory to be "one of the most difficult of the middle grades programmatic components to implement." Anfara summarized current relevant research and noted that many advisories never fulfill the teacher-based guidance aspect of practice. Particularly helpful to the reader is the inclusion of a set of components of successful advisory programs, including various rationales, designs, and emphases.

Galassi, J., Gulledge, S., & Cox, N. (1997). Middle school advisories: Retrospect and prospect. *Review of Educational Research, 67,* 301–338.

In this article, Galassi, Gulledge, and Cox (1997) presented a critical analysis of middle grades advisor-advisee programs and a review of the history and rationale for these programs. The authors offered a typology for distinguishing different advisory programs and a conceptual framework for identifying potential barriers to advisories at the inception as well as the implementation and maintenance phases. They included recommendations to address these barriers and a set of guidelines to improve future research initiatives.

Comprehensive guidance and support services meet the needs of young adolescents. (Guidance Services)

Annotated References

Akos, P., & Kingsley, M. (2008). *Research summary: Middle grades counseling.* Retrieved July 27, 2009, from http://www.nmsa.org/portals/0/pdf/research/Research_Summaries/Counseling.pdf

In this research summary, Akos and Kingley illustrated how the school counselor role has evolved and highlighted the implications of contemporary research and best practices for developmentally responsive middle grades counseling. Drawing upon the American School Counselor Association's (2005) national model, the authors examined the elements of counseling that are supportive of the philosophy and goals of the middle school.

American School Counselor Association. (2005). *The ASCA national model: A framework for school counseling programs, Second Edition.* Alexandria, VA: Author.

American School Counselor Association. (2005). Special issue: Focus on middle school counseling. *Professional School Counseling, 9*(2), 95–176.

Because young adolescents go through a variety of changes as they transition into adolescence, it is important that middle grades counseling programs be developmentally responsive. The American School Counselor Association dedicated this special issue of Professional School Counseling to addressing the issues and concepts that make middle grades counseling unique compared to different levels. Articles included in this special issue examine relevant issues and concepts in middle grades counseling, such as developmental assets, young adolescent development, ethnic identity development, academic development and learning, and family involvement.

Health and wellness are supported in curricula, school-wide programs, and related policies. (Health & Wellness)

Annotated References

Mertens, S. B. (2006). *Research summary: Adolescent health, wellness, and safety.* Retrieved March 27, 2009, from http://www.nmsa.org/portals/0/pdf/research/Research_Summaries/Health.pdf

In this research summary, Mertens reported that despite widespread awareness of the importance of adolescent health, wellness, and safety, adolescents' risky behaviors (e.g., alcohol, tobacco, and drug use; unprotected sexual activity) are increasing. Citing recent research, the author revealed, "Adolescents continue to have high rates of morbidity and mortality owing to violence, injury, and mental health disorders." Subsequently, Mertens described briefly Comprehensive School Health Programs, recommended by the CDC (i.e., Centers for Disease Control), and identified components of Comprehensive School Health Programs: (a) health education; (b) physical education; (c) health services; (d) nutrition services and policies; (e) mental health—counseling, psychological, and social services; (f) healthy school environment; (g) parent and community engagement; and (h) health promotion for faculty and staff.

Schultz, J. (2005). School-wide efforts and policies that foster health, wellness, and safety. In T. O. Erb (Ed.), *This we believe in action: Implementing successful middle level schools* (pp. 153–163). Westerville, OH: National Middle School Association.

Schultz highlighted the importance of health promotion for young adolescents and references recent research findings that underscore its continued need. Shultz suggested three broad reasons to promote wellness (i.e., poor health practices drain resources from education; behavioral, physical, and emotional problems interfere with learning; youthful choices affect health), which she based on numerous governmental reports and research studies. She concluded with ways communities, schools, and individuals can respond to young adolescents' health and wellness needs.

The school actively involves families in the education of their children. (Family Involvement)

Annotated References

Epstein, J. L. (2008). Improving family and community involvement in secondary schools. *The Education Digest, 73*(6), 9–12.

Epstein noted that students benefit from both family and community involvement at the secondary level—middle school and high schools. She found that parents and community members want information—more and better information—on ways to support adolescents. In her section on partnership programs, Epstein called for linking annual plans for family and community involvement to the school improvement plan and specific student learning goals. Additionally, she reviewed her framework that outlines six types of parent involvement (i.e., parenting, communicating, volunteering, learning at home, decision making, collaborating with the community).

Musser, P. M. (2004). Listening to the voices of family members, teachers, and community members. *Research in Middle Level Education Online, 27*(2), 1–14. Retrieved July 25, 2009, from http://www.nmsa.org/portals/0/pdf/ publications/RMLE/rmle_vol27_no2_article2.pdf

Based on focus group results, Musser identified relationships across three influential groups for middle grades students' overall growth academically and personally: family, teachers, and community members. She reported that difficulties with those relationships arose from a lack of communication and conflicts in values.

Pate, P. E., & Andrews, P. G. (2006). *Research summary: Parent involvement.* Retrieved July 27, 2009, from ttp://www.nmsa.org/portals/0/pdf/research/ Research_Summaries/Parent_Involvement.pdf

In this research summary, Pate and Andrews provided a definition of and a review of recent research about parent involvement. The summary highlighted Epstein and a colleague's study of parent involvement in the middle grades and their recommended framework that specified six types of parent involvement (i.e., parenting, communicating, volunteering, learning at home, decision making, collaborating with the community). This research summary also referenced Fan and Chen's (2001) meta-analysis, which advanced similar constructs of parent involvement: (a) communication, (b) supervision, and (c) parental expectations and parenting style. The final sections of the summary list the outcomes of parent involvement and offer suggestions for increasing it.

Fan, X. T., & Chen, M. (2001). Parental involvement and students' academic achievement: A meta-analysis. *Educational Psychology Review, 13,* 1–22.

The school includes community and business partners.

(Community & Business)

Annotated References

Sanders, M. (2001). The role of "community" in comprehensive school, family, and community partnerships. *The Elementary School Journal, 102*(1), 19–34.

In this article, Sanders examined the different roles and conceptions of "community" in school-based family and community partnerships. The author offered different conceptualizations of school-community partnerships, identified gaps in knowledge in the field, and analyzed survey data from more than 400 schools to learn about the kinds of partners that schools collaborate with, particularly on the challenges schools face in developing partnerships with different actors in the community.

Simon, B. S., & Epstein, J. L. (2001). School, community, and family partnerships: Linking theory to practice. In D. B. Hiatt-Michael (Ed.), *Promising practices for family involvement in schools* (pp. 1–24). Greenwich, CT: Information Age.

In this chapter, Simon and Epstein provided readers with a basis for organizing and integrating research on partnerships between schools, families, and elements of the broader community in which they reside. The authors brought together current research on specific ways that family and community influences can benefit student outcomes, reviewed the state of knowledge, and explained how such activities can help students. Their goal was to articulate ways to help different groups of stakeholders to study and implement partnerships between schools and communities.

Recommended Resources

Carnegie Council on Adolescent Development. (1989). *Turning points: Preparing American youth for the 21ˢᵗ century.* New York: Carnegie Corporation.

Cook, T. D., Herman, M. R., Phillips, M., & Settersten, R. A. (2002). Some ways in which neighborhoods, nuclear families, friendship groups, and schools jointly affect changes in early adolescent development. *Child Development, 73*(4), 1283–1309.

Dinkes, R., Cataldi, E. F., & Lin-Kelly, W. (2007). *Indicators of school crime and safety: 2007* (NCES 2008-021/NCJ 219553). Washington, DC: National Center for Education Statistics, Institute of Education Sciences, U.S. Department of Education, and Bureau of Justice, Statistics, Office of Justice Programs, U.S. Department of Justice.

Epstein, J. L., Sanders, M. G., Simon, B. S., Salinas, K. C., Jansorn, N. R., & Van Voorhis, F. L. (2002). *School, community, and community partnerships: Your handbook for action* (2ⁿᵈ ed.). Thousand Oaks, CA: Corwin.

Fan, X. T., & Chen, M. (2001). Parental involvement and students' academic achievement: A meta-analysis. *Educational Psychology Review, 13,* 1–22.

Mertens, S. B., Anfara, V A., Jr., & Roney, K. (Eds.). (2009.) *An international look at educating young adolescents.* Charlotte, NC: Information Age.

Moje, E. B. (2006). Motivating texts, motivating contexts, motivating adolescents: An examination of the role of motivation in adolescent literacy practices and development. *Perspectives, 32*(3), 10–14.

Olson, K. (2009). *Wounded by school: Recapturing the joy in learning and standing up to old school culture.* New York: Teachers College Press.

Raider-Roth, M. (2005). *Trusting what you know: The high stakes of classroom relationships.* San Francisco: Jossey-Bass.

Reed, D. F., McMillan, J. H., & McBee, R. H. (1995). Defying the odds: Middle schoolers in high-risk circumstances who succeed. *Middle School Journal, 27*(1), 3–10.

Spear, R. C. (2005). *Taking the lead in implementing and improving advisory.* Westerville, OH: National Middle School Association.

Part IV

Middle Grades Research: Future Directions

Research findings, as articulated throughout this book, influence perceptions of the middle school concept as well as middle grades programs and practices. While decades of research support the middle school concept and provide evidence of effectiveness, additional research studies will strengthen the middle grades knowledge base. Middle grades advocates, researchers, and associations (e.g., Anfara et al., 2003; Hough, 2003; Mertens, 2006; NMSA, 1997; Van Zandt & Totten, 1995) are in agreement—our field needs more research.

To continue building the middle grades education research base, we return to the recommendations offered by Anfara and colleagues (2003) in the original *Research and Resources in Support of This We Believe*. Because these six recommendations are still germane, they are worthy of review. After reviewing these, we propose a seventh recommendation to advance our collective goal of expanding the middle grades research base.

First, our field needs more large-scale, longitudinal studies. To influence national educational policies (e.g., No Child Left Behind Act of 2001) as well as regional and state initiatives will require research findings that are reliable and generalizable. Middle grades researchers need to design and conduct large-scale, longitudinal studies that measure the effects of the middle school concept on student performance including academic achievement and socio-emotional development.

Second, our field needs more mixed methods studies. Mixed methods studies incorporate both qualitative and quantitative methodologies, which allow researchers to draw on the inherent strengths and mitigate weaknesses associated with these methods. The combination of these two methodological approaches can lead to benefits such as better triangulation of data, validation of findings, and richer contextual information.

Third, our field needs more studies that examine multiple components of the middle school concept and how these interact within the school environment. To date, the majority of middle grades research has centered on individual components of the middle school concept (e.g., advisory, teaming, school climate, instruction, parent involvement). While the findings from these studies are important and contribute significantly to our understanding of the impact of individual programmatic components on student performance, we need studies that focus on multiple components so that we understand (a) how they relate to one another and (b) the combined effects of multiple components. (See Part Two for studies that examined multiple components of the middle school concept.)

> Cross-disciplinary studies allow researchers to draw on the expertise of multiple disciplines.

Fourth, our field needs to replicate studies. Researchers need to conduct studies that replicate previous methods and designs. For example, researchers would use the same data collection instruments, employ the same data analyses, and report their findings to the educational community. Replicating studies is essential for validating the findings from earlier studies and fortifying the research base.

Fifth, our field needs to more experimental studies—ones that include control groups and random assignment. Though randomization is difficult in educational settings, the U.S. Department of Education and a number of educational foundations support and fund research that employs experimental designs. Results from experimental studies will not only provide additional evidence of effectiveness regarding middle grades education, but they will also allow us to respond appropriately and adequately to critics of the middle school concept.

Sixth, our field needs to establish a national database to address questions about the middle school concept and middle schools. We need to continue efforts to initiate and maintain a national database. Notably, the Middle Level Education Research Special Interest Group (MLER SIG) has taken the first steps toward creating a national database as part of their National Middle Grades Research Program. This national database will be an important source for addressing relevant research questions.

Seventh, our field needs to engage in collaborative research initiatives. These collaborative projects include cross-disciplinary and inter-institutional studies as well as comparative and international research. Cross-disciplinary studies allow researchers to draw on the expertise of multiple disciplines, while inter-institutional studies allow researchers within the same discipline to work collectively. Comparative and international research fosters the development of global communities of scholars and promotes cross-cultural understanding of ideas and issues related to the education of young adolescents. Engaging in collaborative research could broaden our understanding of the middle school concept as well as middle grades practices and programs. We propose this recommendation to advance our goal of expanding the middle grades research base.

References

Anfara, V. A., Jr., Andrews, P. G., Hough, D. L., Mertens, S. B., Mizelle, N. B., & White, G. P. (2003). *Research and resources in support of This We Believe*. Westerville, OH: National Middle School Association.

Hough, D. L. (2003). *R3= Research, rhetoric, and reality: A study of studies*. Westerville, OH: National Middle School Association.

Mertens, S. B. (2006). *A proposal for establishing a national middle level research project.* A research white paper. Retrieved July 27, 2009, from http://www.rmle.pdx.edu/docs/MLERNationalMLProjectWhitePaper.pdf

National Middle School Association. (1997). *A 21st century research agenda: Issues, topics, & questions guiding inquiry into middle level theory & practice.* Columbus, OH: Author.

No Child Left Behind Act of 2001, Pub. L. No. 107–110, 115 Stat. 1425 (2002).

Van Zandt, L. M., & Totten, S. (1995). The current status of middle level education research: A critical review. *Research in Middle Level Education Quarterly, 18*(3), 1–25.

CPSIA information can be obtained at www.ICGtesting.com
Printed in the USA
BVOW062013240413

319066BV00002B/5/P